CW00818953

THE ULTIMATE *Mom* CHALLENGE

From Gray Area Drinking to Sober and Free

Celeste Yvonne

*A COMPILATION OF CELESTE YVONNE'S
MOST POPULAR, FREQUENTLY SHARED AND OFTEN REQUESTED
STORIES TO BRING YOU INSPIRATION & HOPE*

FROM THE AUTHOR

WHY THIS BOOK?

"What if I compiled all my best pieces on addiction and recovery and created a survival guide to help others?"

These were my thoughts last night as I lay with my son in bed while he drifted off. My writing has been seen by over 50 million people on Facebook alone. Collectively, there are so many things to tell you; things that just one post or article doesn't do justice.

So I've compiled them. For you.

My words into your hands, and ultimately, hopefully into your heart.

If you are on a sober journey, sober curious, or if you are supporting a loved one who is struggling, I want you to know there is hope. I found more in my sobriety than I ever could find in the bottom of a wine glass.

Genetics were against me; mommy wine culture was against me... but I overcame the lure of alcohol.

You can too.

THE ULTIMATE Mom CHALLENGE

CHAPTER 1

I'M A MOM WHO SELF-MEDICATES, AND IT'S COMPLICATED

THIS IS THE FIRST PIECE I EVER WROTE WHERE I GOT HONEST ABOUT MY UNHEALTHY DRINKING.

Do you self-medicate? I do.

After a long day at home or a stressful day at work, I definitely feel like I earned that glass of wine at dinner. Sometimes when I've gone a few nights with little sleep, I'll pop a Tylenol PM to move things along. Is this terrible? Am I well on the path to AA?

I'm pretty sure I'm not alone here. You can't scroll through Facebook or Twitter without at least one joke tying mothers to wine-drinking or stressed-out women on the verge of a breakdown. They pretty much promise that wine is the answer to all their problems. I love these memes and funny tweets too, because I can surely relate. Sometimes the only thing I've got going for me after a particularly horrific day is the assurance of that delicious glass of wine waiting for me after the kids' bedtime.

I read an enlightening article in *The Atlantic* about how moms self-medicating with booze has become so common and so ingrained in our society that we don't even realize how unhealthy a habit it is and what it inevitably leads to. The article says that in the '70s and '80s, pop culture promoted pill popping more than booze. But since they discovered that pills like Vicodin are ridiculously addictive and dangerous, society has shifted to the ever-present wino momma.

The article delves deeper into why we need to self-medicate in the first place. The pressure we are putting on ourselves to be all things is so overbearing, so unsustainable, that we need that release just to survive. I believe it. Some days, I'm so wound up by the end of the day, I get nauseous to the point where I think I'll throw up. Other days, I'll get headaches the size of boulders crushing my skull.

Last night, I lost my mind around 7:18 p.m., just as I was giving my son a bath and getting him ready for bed. I felt myself physically shut down. When my husband saw the look on my face, he promptly took over bedtime duties and told me to go lie down. He's seen that look before. It's not pretty.

What's a mom to do? Last night, I went to bed at 7:30 p.m. because I could. But I can't do that every night. Normally nighttime is prime time for getting the kids' lunches ready for school the next day, washing the dinner dishes, moving the clothes from the washer to dryer so they aren't all mildewy by morning, and paying bills — because even after my mommy duties end each night, my responsibilities as an adult remain.

So, on the days when going to bed at 7:30 isn't an option, sometimes I break out a wine glass instead. The best part is I can enjoy the wine and feel like I'm treating myself, while still getting my obligations done at the same time. Self-medicating? Boo. But multitasking? Hooray! It feels even better because I'm not being completely selfish and directing all my time and attention on me and relaxation. It feels like something a responsible mom who wants to wind down would do.

But as if moms don't feel guilty enough, now we need to feel guilty about this luxury too. I understand the reasons, but I still feel myself scream inside, "No, people! Don't take this from us too!"

I cannot deny that I let that guilt chip away at me. Addiction is a strong force in my family history. I remind myself of that with every sip. Can I still enjoy this pleasure while that truth tugs at me? Am I playing with fire every time I pop open a cork?

And if I do put the wine glass down, do I need to find a different, healthier way to self-medicate? Perhaps. Or do I need to find a less stressful way of living altogether? Kick the root cause out the door. But seriously, I don't know how realistic that is. In this world where parents are super-human caretakers, breadwinners, Pinterest fiends, and PTA members, we are expected to do it all while sporting six-pack abs. No excuses — unless you want to be "that" mom: the mom who other people whisper about, who can't get her act together, doesn't seem that engaged in her children's passions, or never seems to have her priorities in order.

Now that's a stigma I never want to have.

CHAPTER 2

I'M A WINO MOM

I WROTE THIS ON MY DAY 1. I WAS SICK AND TIRED OF FEELING SICK AND TIRED. IT WAS THE END OF AN ERA, AND THE START OF A WHOLE NEW LIFE. BUT THAT DAY I WAS SO SCARED. TERRIFIED. I WISH I COULD GO BACK AND TELL MYSELF EVERYTHING WOULD BE OK.

I'm a wino mom, for sure. A glass of Merlot as soon as the clock strikes five. By bedtime, the bottle's empty and I'm either drunk or damn close. Some nights are better than others. If I have a big day scheduled for the next day, I'll take it slow or hold off altogether. But other nights, the goal is to get drunk. Period.

Don't play that "glass of wine or two" shit with me. I don't even want to drink if that's all I can have. This booze thing... it's a tease, it's a game, it's a journey to see how much I can drink without other people noticing or me collapsing on my bed — whichever comes first.

But am I an alcoholic?

I don't drink every day. And when I'm alone with the kids I don't drink at all. I always wait till after 5 pm to start, and I'm in bed by 9... hoping to sleep everything off by morning.

But some mornings after heavy drinking are rough. Really rough. I get out of bed because I have to, but it hurts. My head is pounding, my stomach is weak. I have to face the day because I have kids to take care of, whereas back in the day I could sleep the nausea off. A day of plans — errands, chores at home, activities with the kids — often turns into a day of nursing my wounds and pushing things off until tomorrow.

But am I an alcoholic?

My dad was an alcoholic. He started drinking beer before 9 am. He transitioned to gin by the afternoon. He was taking us kids to school, driving us home and to vol-leyball practice. He was hiding his booze in the dresser, the cabinet, under the sofa... When his jig was up, even he was the first one to tell you he was a raging alcoholic and he wanted to stay that way.

I drink wine like seemingly every Facebook mom on earth. I self-medicate to get through the kid tantrums, the pressure to do and have it all, and the utter boredom of being at home all damn day. I am somewhat "responsible," never driving under the influence, keeping my inebriation in check most of the time. But I track time by when my next drink will be. On Thursday, at the networking party? Or on Saturday, when my husband and I have a date night? And when the drinking starts, my only concern is where I will get my next glass. Can I order another drink now? Or should I wait till we get home. I'm on a hunt, and I'm hungry for more, always more. There is never a "that's enough" feeling. It's only when my eyes fade to black that I am done.

My health is in check. My vitals are all good. I eat a lot of kale and I work out daily. But still, this almost-daily drink obsession is destroying my life. It eats at me, demanding more more more all night and feeding my guilt and shame in the morning. It holds me back from being a great mom, wife, friend, and person and limits my opportunities to do great things — for myself, for my family, for our future.

But all my friends drink wine. We all joke about "wine o'clock". We meet for girls' night and pound wine like it's about to go bad. Everything's more fun with booze, and the perils of parenting go from exhausting and isolating to hilarious and revelatory. Surely we can't all be alcoholics.

We're just women who need a break. I'm just a mom who needs an outlet.

I'm smart, I'm active, and I have a family who loves me. I have people around me who I love dearly, and they could potentially leave me if I can't get my act together. I have little kids who count on me for their survival and need me to be secure, focused, and sober.

But am I an alcoholic?

A resounding yes. And recovery starts now.

CHAPTER 3

I THOUGHT I WAS DYING.
TURNS OUT, I WAS TAKING MY FIRST STEP
TOWARDS RECOVERY.

The question I always get from people who've read about my alcohol recovery is "How did you start?"

And I get why. Every journey begins with the first step. And, for so many of us, the first step is terrifying.

I do not attend AA, but I understand their mantra, "One day at a time" with every part of me. Because that is how my recovery began. It's how everyone's recovery begins—the one day that changes everything.

My story starts on a melancholy Monday in December of 2017. It was the third week of the month, with weeks of holiday party hangovers under my belt. And I was just getting started. The holidays were especially triggering for me as all my family came to town, the beer tap opened, and champagne started popping.

I sat at my computer at work, nursing a subtle hangover. Hangovers were common for me, and although the previous evening's party wasn't particularly boozy, my body was recovering from three consecutive days of drinking.

Not that I ever needed a party as an excuse to drink. Drinking felt earned for pretty much everything: stress, boredom, parenting struggles. I got very good at finding reasons to drink.

And year after year, my drinking seemed to grow steadier, stronger, and more determined as if it had a mind of its own. The days of wine with friends now started with wine before meeting with those friends and wrapped with a nightcap. When you start drinking like this, you have to start getting sneaky. Two glasses of wine? No one bats an eyelash. But a night during which people only saw me drink two glasses in front of them was easily a four-glass night.

Because four? People start whispering. And, as I approached my 40th birthday, the goal was to minimize whispers. The strategy was to be sneaky. And it worked like a charm.

That day, I sat in my office chair and felt my heart flutter like it was skipping beats. I put my hand to my chest and could feel it: bu-dum... bu-dum... pause... bu-dum.

Panic set in fast. I knew something was very wrong and I was certain that I was having a stroke. I was 38 years old, and I was having a stroke.

This self-diagnosis sounds extreme, I know. But it's important that you know that my father, a serious alcoholic, suffered from a debilitating stroke at 52. My dad—the most athletic, handsome, life-of-the-party guy—almost lost his life at a young 52. And although he didn't die that day, he was permanently disabled.

The first day was the hardest, of course. Explaining my ER trip to my husband was brief and awkward. But he was supportive. Completely supportive.

The next few days were just as hard as Christmas came and the relatives swarmed with no clue about the battle I was fighting in my head. I tried to go on as if nothing had changed, but, inside, I just wanted to lay in bed and drug myself to sleep with Tylenol PM until the holidays passed and things settled down. On New Year's Eve, we even went out with friends, much to my chagrin.

"Aren't you drinking?" my friend asked as several bottles for the table were ordered.

"No," I said. "I'm taking a break."

Surprised, she responded, "You picked a bad day to take a break. We just ordered some amazing wine."

And maybe I did pick a bad time to quit drinking—although what would be a "good" time? But there's never a bad time to quit drinking. Now is the best time to quit drinking.

I remember that evening, white-knuckling the table while everyone around me drank and drank. I remember everything. I drove my husband and me home safely. I went to sleep and slept well. I even woke up with energy and clarity. I was two weeks into my sober journey but waking up that New Year's Day actually felt like the first day of my new life.

Once I got through those first few weeks of sobriety, I went full-throttle, and I haven't looked back. I'm determined to never start back at day one. I will never go back to day one.

And for the people who ask me how I started, I tell them the first step was to tell someone who would hold me accountable. "I think I am an alcoholic," I said to my mother that strange day in the ER.

The first step was telling my mom.

CHAPTER 4

THE FIRST WEEK
AFTER YOU QUIT DRINKING

Someone asked me to write about that first week after I quit drinking. I've been trying to gather my thoughts on that experience even just to remember for myself because I will admit there's a deep fog around my memory of that week. I did not write during that week. I checked my social media to get an indication of my headspace and I don't have anything posted for that week either. It was like I crawled into a hole and hid away, waiting for the courage to come back out.

That first week was, from memory, the hardest week of my life. But not for the reasons you'd think. I didn't experience any severe withdrawal, though I understand some do. Since I didn't drink every day anyway, my body had no problem adjusting to a week of sobriety. The first week was mentally hard though. The constant mind games were undoubtedly what throws people off those first few days. You would think our bodies would want sobriety. And they do. Our bodies expend so much energy trying to take care of us, even as we sabotage them at every turn. But our brains have other plans. And this first week? Our mind is our worst enemy. You can start this next week. It's been a hard day. Try this tomorrow, not today. You went two days without a drink last week. Obviously you don't have a problem. Everyone else is drinking; why can't you?

On and on and on my mind would drone. Constant chatter trying to throw me off my game. Honestly, I look back now and realize it was a miracle I got through it. I realize now, that I probably didn't write about it for fear I would convince myself not to go through with it. I believed I couldn't trust myself.

But after that first day of sobriety — Day One — I told myself I never have to do that again. Each day I reminded myself that last day was over. I would never have to do it again. And that was my "trick" for getting through that first week. Promising myself that by sticking it out, I was one day closer to freedom. Because every day gets easier. Every day feels freer.

What made my first week exponentially harder was my decision to do this on my own. Only two people knew my decision to quit drinking, and I kept it from everyone else. Instead of giving me their support and love, people were unknowingly testing me with every offer to get me a drink (it was the week of Christmas to make matters even harder), with holding their wine glass close enough that I could practically smell the tannins, and with asking why I wasn't drinking. In that first week, I didn't yet know what my answer was. I didn't quite understand what my long-term plans were.

Is this forever? Is this just a test? Do I have a problem, or do I just need to get better at moderation? So I lied. I told people I was sick. Or I was doing a cleanse. I had to assure a few people I wasn't pregnant, but even then, at that time I would rather someone suspected I was pregnant than have them think I had a drinking problem. Because back then, having a drinking problem or being considered an alcoholic was by far the worst of outcomes. It meant there was something wrong with me. That I was incapable of drinking a perfectly safe beverage that was non-problematic for 90% of the population.

I have learned so much since I quit. I quit on the pretense that alcohol was not serving me, and I couldn't keep drinking without serious implications, either now or in the future. But since I've started reading and learning more about alcohol, and alcohol addiction, I've learned that alcohol isn't safe for anyone — it is addictive in nature, and it's a type one carcinogen that can cause cancer even from low to moderate drinking. I've learned that alcohol addiction is something anyone is susceptible to — not just a subset of the population. But most importantly, I've learned how to trust myself.

For the first time in my life, I have faith in the woman I am and the voice inside of me telling me who I am and why I matter. Alcohol lied to me for so many years, there was a time I didn't know WHO was speaking — Celeste or alcohol? To be able to trust myself and my body again, there are no words to describe the power of that metamorphosis for me, in my life.

I also learned the beautiful skill of setting boundaries. I know what I will and will not put up with. I've learned to say no to people and things that are not beneficial or healthy. I've learned who is here for me, and who just liked me because I was a drinking buddy. Setting boundaries was a skill I could only learn in sobriety.

If I could go back and do that first week all over again, here's what I would do: 1) I would read *This Naked Mind* and *Quit Like a Woman*, both are books which emphasize the harmful addictive nature of alcohol and why it makes quitting so damn hard for EVERYONE, not just "alcoholics." 2) I would find a community, either through Sober Mom Squad, AA or through the myriad of other programs out there. 3) I would search Facebook for one of the many supportive, private communities for sober women. 4) I would avoid parties or any social gatherings that involved alcohol (since I quit over Christmas, this would have been decidedly harder. But I would have set more boundaries… something I'm much better at now, at several years sober.).

I think I did my first week sober the absolute hardest way possible — alone. I would encourage anyone looking to see what sober life feels like to do these four things instead. You do not have to do this alone if you don't want to. This may be the hardest week of your life, but if you are anything like me, you will stay resilient by knowing you never have to do it again. And it's worth it. It's worth all of it.

ONE YEAR LATER

I know what you're thinking. "Wait, what?"

You can't just skip the first year!

Well, sadly I did. I did not write a single thing about my recovery for the first year. I was afraid of giving my feelings power. I was afraid of sparking triggers. And I was deeply afraid of telling people about my decision to quit drinking. Because — well — what if I changed my mind later?

If I could go back, I would certainly do some things differently. But I can't. So, it was on the one-year anniversary of my sober date that I decided to tell the world. I felt happy, settled and free. And I wanted to share the news that quitting alcohol is the opposite of QUITTING.

CHAPTER 5

*I HAD TO SOBER UP TO BE THE MOM
I WANTED TO BE*

Today is a big day. It's the one-year anniversary of the day I decided I'd had enough. I put the bottle down. I sobered up. What? You didn't know about my struggles with alcohol? Does this change your perspective of me? As a woman? As a mom? This used to matter to me. What you thought about me used to mean everything. And in truth, it still does a little. I've kept this part of myself under the radar for fear of judgement… shame… stigmatization.

I don't know a lot of things. I don't know how to stop at one drink. I don't know when to say, "No thanks, I've had enough." But I do know I'm better off with none at all. I do know my family is stronger, happier, and safer when I'm sober. I do know I can wake up fresh and hangover free. I do know my life is more enriched and beautiful when I'm sober.

Is it hard? Of course it is. There were so many tests this year. Breaking a 20+ year habit is hard. I used to drink when I was happy, I drank when I was sad. I drank when I was anxious, and I drank when I was bored.

I drank to socialize. I drank to hide. I drank to numb. I drank to feel secure.

Now I don't drink at all. I've had to find other coping mechanisms. But I've also had to do it cared. I've had to feel the feelings... all the feelings I used to drink to escape from. I can no longer hide.

But this is life! This is what it's all about! It's feeling the feelings. It's doing the shit that scares you. It's feeling terrified and standing up and stepping out anyway.

Do you know what the greatest part about this past year has been? The release of guilt. The elimination of alcohol-related regret. I no longer wake up with regrets. I no longer look at my kids with the guilt of a mom who drinks to numb the stress of parenting.

The stress of them. The stress of this life I have brought them into.

I'm no saint. I still do stupid shit. I yell at my kids. I lose it pretty often, actually. But to parent without the alcohol-fueled buzz? This is priceless to me. I'm a better mother without alcohol. I'm a better wife. I'm a better person.

Can you stop at just one drink? I envy you. Do you linger over your glass of wine and feel satisfied, and say "no thanks" when you're offered more? I can only imagine. This is not me, and it will never be me. I will never reach a time or place where I can moderate my drinking. I know this now. It's been a long, harrowing journey but I know this more deeply than anything I've ever known.

I used to think alcohol served me in some way. It no longer does. It served a different person. A person who wasn't strong enough, wasn't ready to feel everything. To be everything. I'm not that girl anymore. I've never been stronger. I'm ready to feel again.

But I'm no superwoman. In many ways, I've never been weaker. I know alcohol is my kryptonite. I know I'm one drink away from a binge. I know I'm one poor decision away from a lifetime of regret. And I'm so weak, I know I cannot touch booze. I know I must feel again. I have to feel everything again.

I feel good today. Sobriety suits me. I don't feel good every day though, and I still glance twice when the person next to me orders a Cab or Merlot. Maybe I always will. But I never want to go back to day one. I never want to start this journey over again. The first day of recovery is the hardest. Today is day 365, and every day gets better. I promise.

Do you struggle to stop at one? Do you know in your heart you have a problem but don't know where to start or when it's time to stop? I have something amazing to tell you. You can change your life today — right now — for the better. Don't wait for rock bottom. Don't wait until your health deteriorates, or you're drunk when you're driving your kids somewhere, or your spouse leaves you. Beat alcohol to the punch and change your life today.

It will be the hardest day of your life. It will also be one of the greatest. It will be the day you decide to feel again. It will be the day you decide to take back control of your life. It will be the day you can see your kids and partner with a focus and intention you've never experienced before. You will never regret it.

CHAPTER 6

ALCOHOL IS THE ONLY DRUG WE HAVE
TO EXPLAIN WHY WE'RE NOT USING IT

I went to a playdate the other day at someone's house. Almost the moment I stepped through the front door, the mom giggled and announced, "Mimosa time!" and my body froze up.

I wasn't prepared for this.

Most times, when I'm heading to a social gathering, I have time to prepare. I mentally prepare, I physically pre- pare (I always bring a kombucha with me), I emotionally prepare.

I think about what I will say when someone asks why I'm not drinking. I think about how deep into the con- versation I want to get — because some days I'm ready to go there, and other days I want to talk about anything BUT that.

Today, because I was so caught off guard, I probably looked like a deer in headlights. I almost said "Yes" and thought about just pretending to sip it. But I said, "Not right now, I'm good thank you" and the conversation veered to something else.

But it came up again about 15 minutes later. And again another 15 minutes later. And I was practically banging my head against the wall mentally thinking, "why don't I just tell her I don't drink?"

But I didn't. I was afraid she would think I wasn't fun. I was afraid she wouldn't want to have more playdates with us.

I read a meme yesterday that said, "I determine my kids' playdates by which mom I want to drink wine with."

Being alcohol free can truly feel ostracizing. And it's strange to think that alcohol is the only drug that we have to explain why we're NOT using it.

Time to change the narrative. Alcohol free is a choice that should not require an explanation, embarrassment or fear of condemnation.

CHAPTER 7

TO THE PERSON ASKING HERSELF
IF SHE IS AN ALCOHOLIC

I want to tell you a story about a young woman.

She was successful and thriving, happily married with two precious children.

She rocked her professional goals, woke up at 5 am to do hot yoga and was training for a marathon.

She had a toxic relationship with alcohol.

She could stop at a glass of wine but never wanted to. So she would drink and drink some more. Some nights she'd finish a whole bottle of wine by herself. Other nights she wouldn't drink at all.

She found that overall, she was drinking more and more. And overall, she woke up more mornings with headaches than not, as well as a dull achy hangover, and an all-around feeling of anxiety, exhaustion and mild depression.

Was this woman an alcoholic?

IT DOESN'T MATTER.

At the end of the day, alcohol did not serve her. She realized she had a toxic relationship with alcohol and so she quit completely.

She never had another hangover again. She regained the trust of her spouse and kids. She regained control of her life as a whole.

And that is all that matters.

**This is my story. I am 40 years old and two years sober. I quit drinking and I found a freedom that I could never have found from a glass or bottle. People ask me if I'm an alcoholic, and I understand the desire to label. But my response to them and my answer to you is: IT DOESN'T MATTER. Call it what you want. When you realize something doesn't serve you, you need to put it down. Remove the rock from your shoe. And if it's the label that is keeping you from quitting, you are asking yourself the wrong question.

CHAPTER 8

WE PUT SO MUCH ON MOTHERS' PLATES,
IT'S NO WONDER THEY TURN TO WINE

Earlier this year, a post went viral that bemoaned the paradox of modern motherhood: "Go back to work 6-8 weeks after having the baby... Also, breastfeed for at least a year... Also, lose that baby weight..."

I think every mom who read that piece could nod their head in agreement. Being a mom in 2020 is not just hard, it's relentless. There are so many mixed messages between putting family first but also practicing self-care. Don't forget date night. Only buy organic. And if you're not putting money into your retirement at 30, it's basically too late.

We are tired.

We are confused.

We are so anxious.

We are desperate.

Women are drinking more than ever. But is anyone surprised? Between the mental load women carry and the day-to-day stressors to be all and do all, women need an outlet. They need a way to unwind, unload, and relax.

I was one of them. For a long time, I relied on wine to cool off after a day of being a career mom. But according to Joseph Nowinski, PhD, and author of *Almost Alcoholic*, "Drinking has a tendency to escalate – one glass turns into two and then three." Soon, I was regularly pouring that third glass; sometimes finishing the whole bottle myself.

I'm in marketing so I know that what the alcohol industry is doing is brilliant. They are offering mothers a "solution." They've been looking for ways to increase female consumption for years, and now they've got a hook, line and sinker by targeting moms specifically.

They tell us wine is the answer. They tell us wine is good for us. And their messaging reverberates across the social atmosphere. Wine is the antidote to parenting struggles (according to the media). Kids are the reason mommy drinks wine (according to social media).

What the alcohol industry and your social media memes don't tell you is alcohol is a depressant. It actually makes anxiety and depression worse over time. Which is completely counterintuitive to the ads of people looking so happy and carefree as they drink their prosecco and laugh with friends. Or the mom sipping wine while looking on adoringly at her kids playing perfectly together.

Moms, we need to find a better outlet for our stress. We need to reach for something that is not addictive and cancer causing. Something that is not a class one carcinogen.

I sound like a buzz kill. Literally. But guess what? There is a better life without the buzz. I'm living proof. Two years alcohol free and I've never felt, looked or lived better. Take that, wine industry.

It's time for a massive reality check, mamas. I want to see an ad that shows what being a wino mom really looks and feels like: premature aging, massive headaches, and low energy.

An ad with a mom on her third glass of wine — still stressed but drunk on top of it — scrolling through Facebook begrudgingly while her kids play on their iPads because mom is out of energy and out of f*cks.

No one talks about what living sober looks and feels like. You don't see any memes that say, "My kids are the reason I stay sober." But they should exist, seeing those would be a game changer for many people who need to hear that message.. Because being sober is the best thing I've ever done, for my kids and for me.

But don't expect to see that ad anytime soon. Sober doesn't sell the bottles now, does it?

CHAPTER 9

TRANSFORMATION IS AN INSIDE JOB

A transformation rarely looks like it does in the movies. Sometimes, it's an epiphany. A mental shift. Or waking up one morning deciding you are sick of wallowing in your own self-destruction.

For me, I knew something had to change.

I was a mess.

Not on the outside.

On the outside, I looked like I had it all. Husband, kids, great job.

Social media showed the best of me. Vacations, selfies, #thislife, #blessed.

But on the inside, I was falling apart. My anxiety had never been worse. I was growing more fearful and worried about things that didn't used to bother me.

And through it all, I was drinking to cope. It was the only time during the day when I felt relaxed. Relieved. Mommy needs wine right? Only it wasn't a funny meme. It had become a scary reality for this mom.

I was drinking 3,4,5 glasses of wine a night, and waking up the next morning with massive hangovers, shaky hands, and memory lapses. Did I really send that text, or was that just a dream? Did I actually trip and fall in the living room, or did I just imagine it?

I would scan my phone. Texts, calls, social media. What did I write? Please tell me I didn't post anything after 9 p.m.

I always knew that someday I would have to quit drinking. One glass was never enough but a bottle of wine (or more) wasn't sustainable.

On the outside I looked fine, but on the inside I felt like crap. I knew something would have to give. And I realized I could make this decision on my own accord, or the decision would eventually be made for me. And at what cost? What would I have to lose to get to that point? Potentially?

Everything…

So I quit. I quit drinking one cold December morning. I was scared.

Terrified, actually. But I was even more scared of what was going to happen if I didn't quit.

It took me a year to find my sober footing. It was on my one-year anniversary of being sober that I resolved to never drink again. Life is too good sober. I didn't want to miss another minute due to a blackout, to a painful hangover, or to the mounting anxiety.

And I never will.

CHAPTER 10

MY FAVORITE PARENTING MOMENTS DO NOT INCLUDE ALCOHOL

My favorite moments of parenting were never the wine soaked half memories of what may or may not have happened at the birthday party, the playdate or the mimosa fueled brunch.

I do not look back on any of the hard times, when I struggled with PPD and anxiety and couldn't sleep more than a few hours at a time, and wish I drank more.

I can never go back and relive some of my babies' firsts: first steps, first words, first time they blew me a kiss — and experience them sober. I can't go back and feel the natural joy and euphoria of those precious moments without a few glasses of wine dulling my senses.

Nor can I recall the frustrations, the inner rage of trying to connect my old self to this new one, the old life with my unrecognizably exhausting mom existence

— and wonder for even a second if more alcohol might have helped.

Despite all the credit we give alcohol to helping us "survive" parenting, I can truly look back and appreciate 0% of the role it played in my motherhood. You will never hear me wish I drank more to survive the challenges of parenting. Because, in truth, it only took away..

And for all the time, money, and energy I spent convincing myself that "mommy needs wine" to appreciate the milestones, I am left with fuzzier memories and ample regrets. And as mothers we deserve so much more than that. So do our children.

CHAPTER 11

ALCOHOL IS NOT REQUIRED TO HAVE A GOOD TIME

I attended a kid's birthday party for someone in my son's pre-kindergarten class. It was at a trampoline park, and it was every bit the chaos you would expect with 20 five-year-olds running around and literally bouncing off the walls.

The host mom started to coyly pass out drinks to the parents amidst the chaos. It looked like orange juice, but she was giving winks and head nods that this was just for the moms and dads. Having quit drinking a while back, I declined but in years past I would have made a beeline to her the second I heard the words "mommy juice."

In the past, the idea of alcohol at a kid's birthday party never made me think twice. Why can't parents have fun at their kid's parties? After all, we are doing all the work and it's as much a celebration for us as it is for them. It wasn't until three years ago, when I quit drinking for good, that I realized alcohol has infused itself into everything. It's at every party. Every picnic. Every social gathering has a wine bar or keg and a line going halfway down the block of people eager to partake.

And it makes me wonder, what kind of message does this send to our kids? That alcohol is critical to a good time? That a party isn't complete without booze? Maybe. And as someone who realizes I have a toxic relationship with alcohol, that is absolutely the opposite message of what I want my kids to learn about how to have fun.

Anyway, back to the birthday party. Do you see where this is all going? The host mom eventually moved on to other things and left the drinks unattended — and unlabeled but these kids were five anyway, so they weren't exactly proficient at reading — on a table by the cake. At least one kid got his hands on a cup before anyone noticed the table was unattended, but it was too late. That poor little kid was probably sick for the rest of the day.

I'm not judging. I'm guilty, too. I remember serving beer (to the adults, obvs) at my son's third birthday and we all had a blast. But would we have had a great time minus the booze? Of course. And maybe we would be sending a better message to our kids that alcohol is not central to a good time or celebration.

I know I struggle with addiction, and I know it's something that my family has struggled with for generations. I would be ignorant to think my kids won't face similar issues, and my only hope in life is to prepare them as best I can. Not with ignorance but with knowledge, and tools.

Alcohol is not essential to have a good time — let's normalize social events that are alcohol free. Celebration is not interchangeable with champagne. Life and experiences are not enhanced with alcohol, and we need to change this narrative for ourselves. For our kids.

CHAPTER 12

*DEAR KRISTEN
(AND ALL PARTNERS OF ADDICTS),
AN OPEN LETTER TO KRISTEN BELL (AND
ALL PARTNERS OF ALCOHOLICS/ADDICTS)*

I heard your husband relapsed.

After 16 years of vocal sobriety, Dax Sheppard got honest on his podcast and admitted he lost his way. He had fallen and was going to pick himself up and start again.

I know you're scared. As the daughter of an alcoholic I watched my dad's addiction firsthand. I saw the lies, the deceit and the harrowing journey it put the entire family through. I felt the pain of seeing my dad come home with recovery chips from AA while he secretly drank. I remember thetears to my heart as I heard his promises to do better but had a front row seat as his addiction ripped our family at the seams.

You wonder if you can trust him. You wonder how someone could choose drugs and alcohol over your family. Over YOU. Over your CHILDREN! I thought those same things.

Until one day I found myself in a similar position. When I woke up and realized I was using alcohol as a crutch for the anxiety and depression I carried my whole life. And I understood for the first time that addiction is dangerous because there IS NO choice. And I saw that if I didn't quit drinking, I would follow my father's same path.

I want you and every partner of a person in active addiction or recovery to know that this is so much bigger than a choice. Addiction is a brain altering, biochemical disease that overtakes every bit of willpower and sensibility. And your partner's struggles are not uncommon, they are normal even — because drugs and alcohol are extremely addictive. They are chemically designed to enable addiction. Just because some of you can drink regularly without becoming addicted doesn't make you "stronger," it makes you damn lucky.

I can't fix what you and your family are going through, but I can tell you that you are not alone. I can tell you that Al Anon is a powerful support for families in addiction. And I can tell you that your partner is in deep, immense pain. And if this was as simple as making a choice, they would choose you and their family. EVERY time. Because OF COURSE they would.

I woke up one morning three years ago and wished I could drink instead of raising my children and that is how I knew. I indelibly knew that if I didn't turn this around, I may never have the chance again. And my father watches me now from above with astounding pride. Because it was with him and through him I had the courage to quit and wisdom to know where this road could lead.

I quit because my father's addiction took that choice from him. And I pray that with people like Dax who are ending the stigma of addiction and relapse, more of us can get help and speak up sooner. And I believe we will.

Because although addiction is powerful, so is vulnerability. So are our stories. And Dax knows this, perhaps better than most. We are rooting for you and your family, mama.

You can't change someone else, and you certainly can't fix them. But you can stay strong and brave for your family. You can continue to take care of yourself and give yourself so much grace.

As someone who's been on both sides, there are no winners here. There is no lesser pain, only different. And just as I pray for strength for Dax to get through today sober, I also wish you and your children the strength to continue to love and have hope through the pain.

Because truly, the only thing more tragic than addiction — for both sides — is facing it without hope.

CHAPTER 13

I AM SOBER BECAUSE OF MY DAD

My dad used to walk out front to get the mail each afternoon. I would be in the living room, and I'd hear the heavy front door slam behind him. I knew where he was really going.

Once, I followed him out there. I saw him walk toward the sidewalk and head in the opposite direction of the mailbox. Down the road and past a few houses, he disappeared behind some bushes.

I stood back and waited for him to reemerge. After a few minutes, he did. He came out and headed back towards the mailbox, as I stood behind a car, hiding as my body shook from nerves.

When he was safely out of sight I went to the bushes and started moving branches around. I knew exactly what I was looking for and there they were… two empty gin bottles.

I often looked down on my dad's alcoholism as a character defect. A flaw he was responsible for, and something I would never let happen to me.

Even as I drank more and more.

Even when I started to hide my own drinking from others.

ALCOHOL IS TRICKY LIKE THAT. IT MAKES YOU THINK YOU ARE IN CONTROL EVEN AS YOU START DOING THINGS YOU SWORE YOU NEVER WOULD. EVEN WHEN YOU SAW YOUR LOVED ONES STRUGGLE AND SUFFER BY THE SAME HAND.

I loved my father dearly. I was angry with him for a long time, but when I started to see my own struggles with alcohol, I realized how similar we were. I wonder how long he felt in control of his drinking too. I wonder if he struggled with the same voices in his head constantly justifying his increasingly poor choices.

Nobody chooses alcoholism. Nobody chooses addiction.

I'm lucky in a way. Watching my dad's own self-destruction from addiction was the wakeup call I needed to snap out of it. To realize my "control" over alcohol was a façade. And to quit completely.

My dad's gone and I can no longer hug him or talk to him or just smile and watch his eyes light up like they used to when he saw me enter the room. But I like to think he's watching me proudly right now. I found the strength to quit, because of him and through him. And I will not drink again... not because I'm stronger than him, but because his own story and his impact on my life empowered me to do this for me.

And what a legacy he's left for me and my own children. I get to raise them strong and sober, through him.

Because of him.

CHAPTER 14

IN THIS HEAVY DRINKING CULTURE, WE CAN'T HAVE IT BOTH WAYS

Look, I get it. Addiction and recovery are not "cool." They will never be trending on social media. No one ever aspires to be the chick who writes about addiction and recovery (true story).

People consider addiction a bad thing… it's the opposite of what we want for anyone. It's a sad sad outcome of years of self-abuse, or genetics, or childhood trauma or however you want to approach it.

Recovery? It's taboo too. Because recovery proves someone was an addict to start. Recovery means someone had to "sober up" and get real with a serious problem in their life. Calling someone a drunk or wino can be hearsay, but someone who's in recovery? That's a fact.

And yet, we serve one of the most addictive substances on the planet at every party, at every holiday, at every office social function. And yet, we post memes about needing wine to parent, drinking a pitcher of margaritas to hydrate, lacing our tumbler with vodka to get through our kid's soccer practice. We text champagne emojis when someone does something awesome, and wine emojis when someone's having a hard day.

We play Russian roulette with every single person who decides to drink alcohol (90% of the population) and say, "hope it all turns out well!"

And when it doesn't? When 1 out of 8 Americans realize they cannot drink moderately? We pretend not to stare. It's taboo to discuss. We "hope they get help" and stop inviting them to social events. Hoping they figure it out on their own. On. Their. Own.

Where the hell is the middle ground here? And also, what the hell do we expect? We can't have it both ways. We can't put alcohol in front of a person and cheer them on while they drink but look away when they stumble. Drinking is social until it turns to addiction. Then it's the loneliest thing on earth.

The kicker? When someone speaks publicly about their own struggles with addiction, people don't cheer them on. Instead, they get defensive. They point a finger at them and call them an addict. But it's clearly a "them" problem and not the substance itself. It's not the addictive nature of alcohol's fault... that person is just a drunk or an addict.

Look, I'm not trying to repeal the 21st amendment. I think people have the right to drink, if they want. But we cannot promote alcohol in all things we do but turn our backs on people who struggle. Recovery should not be taboo. People should be able to be loud and proud they don't drink. Or to speak publicly about the fact that they need help, and not have the world turn its back on them.

Let's change the narrative. Let's celebrate sobriety, recovery, and admitting when we need help. It's not something to fear or push back on. It's not something to warrant an eye-roll or laughing emoji. It's a wonderful thing! Recovery and sobriety are someone stepping away from society's assumption we can all drink the same way and doing what is good for them.

And addiction? Let's make it part of the conversation. Let's tell our kids and friends and office mates and the lady in the PTA that insists on serving alcohol at every meeting that addiction doesn't just look like pain and suffering. It can look like a mom with two kids. Or a 20 something with two million followers on social media. And instead of inciting shame when someone admits to the struggle? Let's embrace them with support and love. Let's lean in to their problem with love and offer help.

Basically? Let's do the opposite of what we do now.

CHAPTER 15

WHAT YOU NEED TO KNOW
ABOUT THOSE 3-4 GLASSES OF WINE

Very few people turn into "bottle of wine a night" drinkers overnight. For most of us, it is a very slow, discrete progression. So slow, that by the time we realize we are drinking 3-4 glasses of wine each night, our tolerance is so built up that it doesn't feel dangerous. It doesn't feel unsafe. It feels like we still have control.

That is the danger of addiction. The mind tricks of the drug make our brain think we are still in charge. We are still under control. We are high functioning, we have good jobs, happy relationships, and are raising healthy kids. But we are drinking 3 to 4 drinks a night and can't imagine ourselves going even a whole week without alcohol.

If I was to continue fooling myself, I would have kept telling myself that I just have a high tolerance. My body can handle more alcohol than most. But the numbers don't lie. A bottle of wine a night is not safe for anybody. A bottle of wine is what any addiction specialist would consider high-risk drinking.

I was a problem drinker even though I felt like I was under control. And even though my addictive brain tried to tell me, "It's OK, just look at everything you're doing... you deserve this."

Not to mention, it seems like everyone around me was drinking just as much. It couldn't be that bad if everyone else was doing it too.

And that is part of the problem. We are so surrounded in this active alcohol addiction culture, it's hard not to look around and see other people at the high-risk drinking level who also act and seem like they've got it under control.

Do not let the addictive brain lie to you. 3 to 4 glasses of wine a night is high-risk drinking. It is a dangerous level that leads to severe health problems. At that level, it is not a matter of if, but when.

As a mom of two little kids, I had to make a choice. Did I want to continue this cycle, or did I want to live to see my kids grow up? It sounds extreme. It's not. Each year, 88,000 people die in the U.S. from alcohol related deaths. These deaths are PREVENTABLE.

I chose my kids, my health, my family. But I know how hard it is to turn off that voice in your head that tells you it's OK. I know on paper it seems like an obvious choice, but in real life it's hard as hell.

If you want to make this choice but don't know where to start, there are many resources. Check out books by Holly Whitaker and read *This Naked Mind*. Find a recovery group near you, or even a private group on Facebook. Do a 30-day challenge (Annie Grace has a great one). Tell someone who will hold you accountable but without judgement or shame.

Alcohol is not your friend, despite what society and the alcohol industry try to make you think. And you are no less of a person for falling into this trap. Some of the strongest, smartest, bravest, most incredible people on this planet are standing right beside you. All that matters now is what you do next.

What will you do next?

DO YOU KNOW IN YOUR HEART
YOU HAVE A PROBLEM
BUT DON'T KNOW WHERE
TO START OR WHEN IT'S TIME TO QUIT?

I HAVE SOMETHING AMAZING TO TELL YOU.
YOU CAN CHANGE YOUR LIFE TODAY —
RIGHT NOW — FOR THE BETTER.

RESOURCES FOR YOU:

BOOKS:

QUIT LIKE A WOMAN, HOLLY WHITAKER

THIS NAKED MIND, ANNIE GRACE

WE ARE THE LUCKIEST, LAURA MCKOWEN

HIGHLIGHT REAL, EMILY PAULSON

SHAPE OF A WOMAN, JEN ELIZABETH

NOT DRINKING TONIGHT, AMANDA WHITE

COMMUNITIES

SOBER MOM SQUAD

THE LUCKIEST CLUB

AA

SHE RECOVERS